Artisans Around the World

Scandinavia

Sharon Franklin, Teresa Langness, and Cynthia A. Black

RAINTREE
STECK-VAUGHN
PUBLISHERS
A Steck-Vaughn Company

Austin, Texas

www.steck-vaughn.com

Developed by Franklin Tull, Inc.,
Manager: Sharon Franklin
Designer: Dahna Solar
Maps: Terragraphics, Inc.
Illustrators: Dahna Solar and James Cloutier
Picture Researcher: Mary Tull
Projects: Cynthia A. Black

Raintree Steck-Vaughn Publishers Staff
Project Manager: Joyce Spicer
Editor: Pam Wells
Electronic Production: Scott Melcer

Library of Congress Cataloging-in-Publication Data
Franklin, Sharon.
   Scandinavia / Sharon Franklin, Teresa Langness, and Cynthia A. Black.
      p.   cm. — (Artisans around the world)
   Includes bibliographical references (p.   ) and index.
   Summary: Presents brief historical information about Scandinavia as well as descriptions of the cultures of the people
of Sweden, Denmark, Norway, and the area known as Lapland. Includes instructions for making craft projects
representative of the people.
   ISBN 0-7398-0122-8
   1. Material culture — Scandinavia — Juvenile literature. 2. Folk art—Scandinavia — Juvenile literature. 3. Ethnic art —
Scandinavia — Juvenile literature. 4. Artisans—Scandinavia — Juvenile literature. 5. Scandinavia—Social life and
customs — Juvenile literature. 6. Creative activities and seat work — Juvenile literature. [1. Folk art — Scandinavia.
2. Artisans. 3. Scandinavia — Social life and customs. 4. Handicraft.] I. Langness, Teresa. II. Black, Cynthia A. III. Title.
IV. Series.
GN585.S34F73   2000
306'.0948 — dc21

                                                                                                  98-53099
                                                                                                  CIP   AC

Printed and bound in the United States
1 2 3 4 5 6 7 8 9 0 WO 03 02 01 00 99

Table of Contents

The icons next to the projects in the Table of Contents identify the easiest and the most challenging project in the book. This may help you decide which project to do first.

⇨ easiest project

✪ most challenging project

Introduction to Artisans Around the World

There are many ways to learn about the history and present-day life of people in other countries. In school, students often study the history of a country to learn about its people. In this series, you will learn about the history, geography, and the way of life of groups of people through their folk art. People who create folk art are called **artisans.** They are skilled in an art, a craft, or a trade. You will then have a chance to create your own folk art, using your own ideas and symbols.

What Is Folk Art?

Folk art is not considered "fine art." Unlike many fine artists, folk artisans do not generally go to school to learn how to do their art. Very few folk artists are known as "famous" outside of their countries or even their towns. Folk art is the art of everyday people of a region. In this series, folk art also includes primitive art, that is, the art of the first people to be in an area. But, beware! Do not let this fool you into thinking that folk art is not "real" art. As you will see, the quality of the folk art in this series is amazing by any standards.

Folk art comes from the heart and soul of common people. It is an expression of their feelings. Often, it shows their personal, political, or religious beliefs. It may also have a practical purpose or meet a specific need, such as the need for shelter. In many cases, the folk art in the "Artisans Around the World" series comes from groups of people who did not even have a word for art in their culture. Art was simply what people did. It was a part of being human.

Introduction to *Scandinavia*

In this book, you will learn about these crafts and the people who do them:

Oro mobiles in Sweden

Cross-stitch samplers in Denmark

Magic drums in Lapland

Rosemaling in Norway

Then you will learn how to do projects of your own.

Here are some questions to think about as you read this book:

Did any of these folk arts help to meet specific needs?
If so, in what way?

Which folk arts expressed people's religious, political, or personal views?

Were some of these folk arts traditionally created mostly by men or by women?
Why do you think that was so? Is it still true today?

How did the history of a country influence some folk art traditions?

How did the geography, including the natural resources, of a country
influence some folk art traditions? How did people get folk art materials
that they needed but that were not found in their region?

Do some folk art traditions tell a story about a group of people or a culture?
If so, in what way?

How have these folk art traditions been passed down from generation to generation?

Folk Art Today

Reading about these folk art traditions, as well as creating your own folk art,
will increase your respect for the people who first did them.
Do you think some of these art forms, such as cross-stitching, could be created
faster or more easily using machines, like the sewing machine, or technology, like the computer?
Do you think anything would be lost by doing so, even if it were possible?

All of these folk art traditions of the Scandinavia began long ago.
Can you think of any new folk art traditions being started now, in the
United States or in other countries? If so, what are they?
If not, why do you think there are no new traditions?

Safety Guidelines

These folk art projects are a lot of fun to do, but it's important to follow basic safety rules as you work. Here are some guidelines to help as you complete the projects in this book. Work slowly and carefully. That way you can enjoy the process.

1. Part of being a responsible person of any age is knowing when to ask for help. Some of these projects are challenging. Ask an adult for help whenever you need it. Even where the book does not tell you to, feel free to ask for help if you need it.

2. Handle all pointed tools, such as scissors, in a safe manner. Keep them stored in a safe place when not in use.

3. When painting, protect your clothing with an old shirt or a smock. When wet, acrylic paint can be removed with water. After it dries, it cannot be removed.

By the way, part of being an artist involves cleaning up! Be sure to clean up your work area when you are finished. Also, remember to thank anyone who helped you.

Reindeer live in Lapland, Sweden, above the Arctic Circle.

NORWEGIAN SEA

L a p l a n d

FINLAND

Mt. Kebnekaise

Kiruna

Torne River

Gällivare

Jokkmokk

Arctic Circle

SWEDEN

Angerman River

I n n e r

Vangel River

Umeå

Education is very important to the Swedish people. Learning takes place even on mobile computer lab buses.

N
W · E
S

0   100 miles
0   150 km

NORWAY

N o r t h l a n d

Sundsvall

GULF OF BOTHNIA

Dal River

Gripsholm Castle in Stockholm is a reminder of Sweden's long history.

S w e d i s h

Lake Mälaren

★ **Stockholm**

Lake Vänern

L o w l a n d

Gulf of Finland

ESTONIA

Lake Vättern

Skagerrak

Göteburg

S o u t h S w e d i s h H i g h l a n d

Gotland

LATVIA

Kattegat Strait

Kalmar

Öland

This Viking grave is centuries old. It is a reminder of the Vikings' presence in Sweden during the Middle Ages.

Malmö

BALTIC SEA

DENMARK

LITHUANIA

Sweden

▲ Stockholm is one of Europe's most beautiful cities. It is built on islands connected by bridges.

Sweden Facts

Name: Sweden
(Kingdom of Sweden)
Capital: Stockholm
Borders: Norway, Finland.
A narrow strait separates Denmark and Sweden.
Population: 8,854,322
Language: Swedish
Size: 173,732 sq. mi.
(449,965 sq km)
High/Low Points: Mount Kebnekaise, 6,926 ft. (2,111 m); sea level along the coast
Climate: Southern Sweden has wet winters and cool summers; northern and eastern Sweden get cold Siberian air masses; northern Baltic area remains consistently cold; average temperatures range from 5° F (-15° C) in February to 64° F (18° C) in July
Wildlife: Red deer, red foxes, reindeer, moose, brown bears, lynx; willow grouse, black grouse, sea eagles, wild swans, mute swans, whooper swans; Atlantic salmon, brown trout, northern pike
Plants: Birch, aspen, spruce, pine, oak; plants include mosses, lichens, wildflowers, orchids, grasses, lingonberries

From Cityscapes to Winter Wonderland

Welcome to Sweden! It is a land of interesting extremes. The large cities in southern Sweden have some of the world's most sophisticated museums, shopping areas, artistic performances, and city parks. In fact, Europe chose Stockholm as its center of culture in 1998. Yet, in the northern parts of Sweden, the snow, ice, and reindeer make guests feel as if they are in Santa's hometown.

▲ For the Saami people of Lapland, Sweden, snowmobiles are a practical way of getting from place to place.

Fifty bridges connect Stockholm's 14 islands with the mainland. **Medieval** buildings and modern skyscrapers show the contrast between old and new. Because so many people work in the city, they live in tall apartment buildings. City dwellers get around by car, but farther north, in the frosty wilderness area called Lapland, people often travel by snowmobile.

People and Pastimes

Native-born Swedish people tend to be tall, athletic, and healthy looking. The look of health may be due in part to spending time outdoors, even when the weather is cold. For example, people do not stop fishing when the weather turns cold and the rivers freeze over. They simply cut holes in the ice and fish through the holes.

Swedes are famous for their large athletic competitions. An annual international basketball championship draws participants from 54 countries. Runners from around the world compete in the Stockholm Marathon. Some American runners have called it the world's best event for runners. The racers get to see the sights of Stockholm along the 26-mile (41.8 km) route.

Serious Skiing

Swedish skiers take their sport seriously. Every year, thousands of people participate in a cross-country ski race called the Vasa Race, perhaps named after the Vasa kings. The racers must cover about 55 miles (89 km).

Here for the Long Run

Native-born Swedish people tend to have similar physical features, traditions, and lifestyles. In some parts of the world, **migration** creates a diverse ethnic mix of people and cultures. In Sweden, the people moved in and stayed. Most of them came from Germanic tribes who settled there at the end of the Ice Age. As the last of the glaciers melted, farmers moved into the area and began to grow crops. Their descendants, the Vikings, opened up trade routes along rivers throughout the Middle East, Russia, and Scandinavia, a region that includes Sweden, Norway, Finland, and Denmark.

In recent years, people from other countries like Macedonia have moved to Sweden seeking political and religious freedom. As a result, Sweden is becoming more diverse.

Viking Reminders

The Vikings tried to conquer the lands around the Baltic Sea during the Middle Ages. Sweden and its other Scandinavian neighbors continued to battle one another from the 13th century until 1905. The castles, ruins, rock paintings, and cobblestone streets still bear reminders of those early battles. Tourists still visit Viking fortresses for clues to the past.

A Nation of Peace

As much as the Vikings were known for their will to conquer, modern Swedes are known for keeping peace. Sweden remained neutral in World War I and World War II. The Swedish government now supports peace-keeping bodies, such as the United Nations.

Cobblestone Reminders

Sweden's history lives on in the cobblestone streets that still exist, even in large cities such as Stockholm. Legend has it that Viking horsemen made straw shoes for their horses to muffle the noise of their hooves on the cobblestones when the Vikings attacked at night. Who would have thought that these fierce warriors may have spent their free time braiding and sewing straw?

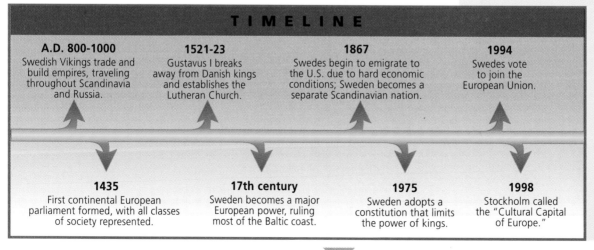

TIMELINE

A.D. 800-1000
Swedish Vikings trade and build empires, traveling throughout Scandinavia and Russia.

1521-23
Gustavus I breaks away from Danish kings and establishes the Lutheran Church.

1867
Swedes begin to emigrate to the U.S. due to hard economic conditions; Sweden becomes a separate Scandinavian nation.

1994
Swedes vote to join the European Union.

1435
First continental European parliament formed, with all classes of society represented.

17th century
Sweden becomes a major European power, ruling most of the Baltic coast.

1975
Sweden adopts a constitution that limits the power of kings.

1998
Stockholm called the "Cultural Capital of Europe."

Nature's Gifts to Sweden

It is easy to see why the first Swedish settlers never wanted to leave. There are breathtaking scenes of rugged mountains laced with snow. Farmland, cities, and beaches lie beyond meadows sprinkled with flowers and dotted with crystal lakes. Wide expanses of forestland, cut by rivers, are also a part of Sweden's landscape.

Sweden's Gifts to the World

Today, Sweden makes good use of its rich natural resources. The country exports beautiful furniture made of wood from Swedish forests. Sweden also produces ships, cars, knives, and tools made from steel. Swedish artisans combine natural materials with their love of fine craftsmanship to create many products. Wood carvings, textiles, sculptures, straw baskets, and ornaments have long decorated Swedish homes. Now they add beauty to homes around the world.

The Swedish people once struggled to earn their living by farming and fishing. When the rest of the Western World began to develop manufacturing a century ago, the Swedes improved their economy by inventing small machines. They developed the first ice-cream maker, modern matches, and a version of the telephone. One of the most famous inventors, Alfred Nobel, created dynamite in the mid-1800s. He did not want to leave such an invention as his only contribution to society, however. With the money he earned, he left a fund for annual awards in areas like physics, chemistry, medicine, and literature. These awards are called the Nobel Prizes. But the prize given for the promotion of international peace is called the Nobel Peace Prize. Each year, the Nobel committee awards prizes to an international scientist, a writer, and a leader for peace whose work has benefited people throughout the world.

Living the "Middle Way"

The Swedish way of life is sometimes called the "middle way," because it combines the best of two types of government—democracy and socialism. People can own land and small businesses. They can think and speak freely, as in a democracy. Yet the Swedish government pays for their education, health care, and, sometimes, housing. In this system, no one suffers from extreme poverty. Sweden protects the well-being of all its citizens, including children. The law does not allow parents to hit or spank their children. All family members have the opportunity to live a healthy life and to learn all they can.

◄ A mannequin dressed in traditional clothing stands next to a dishware display in one of Stockholm's biggest department stores.

◀ In the dim noonday light of midwinter, a dogsled team travels through the snow.

High Country for the Hardy

The beauty of its landscape and way of life make Sweden sound like an ideal place to live. However, only the hardy can endure the dark, cold winters. Sweden's northern tip lies inside the Arctic Circle, in the Land of the Midnight Sun. In the midsummer the sun never sets. In the winter the sun comes out only at midday. People in the mountain areas must walk in the snow for eight months of the year. When the snow ends, the rain begins. Many people prefer the milder but breezier climates of the Swedish Lowland, where most of the farms and cities have developed. Yet even in the milder climates, people expect frequent changes in the weather.

Sharing the Woods

Sweden's lush woods are open to everyone. By law, all people can walk, gather plants, or even camp in the woods without worrying about trespassing, or crossing another person's land. People consider it their duty to take good care of their shared land.

Crafts for the Climate

▲ Early Swedish people found many uses for sedge.

Folk craft traditions often grow out of need. Old Swedish paintings of peasant life suggest that some straw goods came into use as a way of dealing with the weather. People could make stiff straw mats with sedge, a rough-stemmed plant that grows near marshes. The sedge worked well for scraping off the mud when family members trudged in during a wet winter storm.

People used softer straw to make mats for sitting inside by the fire. These mats would protect their bodies from the cold when they sat on the floor. People also made hats to keep the snow and rain off their heads. In southern Sweden, people used straw baskets for carrying goods, both indoors and outdoors.

During the medieval period, Swedes made weather-resistant shoes out of straw. Shaped like Dutch wooden shoes, these straw overshoes protected people's feet as they walked through a wet, spongy area called a bog. The water rushed in, but when the wearer left the bog, the water would quickly drain out.

Straw Handcrafts for Christmas

Grasses that grew well in the summer can be dried and crafted into special holiday decorations. At Christmas time, Swedish families hang a straw star in the window and make straw ornaments for the tree. They hang an *oro*, a crown made of straw, above the table on Christmas Eve. Families spend days preparing a *smorgasbord*, a table full of a wide assortment of food. After Christmas Eve dinner, *Jultomte,* the Christmas **gnome** (or Santa Claus), comes knocking at the door. According to tradition, he has spent all year hiding beneath the floorboards, where he watches and protects the family. This gnome supposedly prefers rice porridge to the meats, fish, salads, and pastries on the table. The children must offer him a bowl of porridge or leave the porridge in the attic stairway at midnight. Then he will open his bag of gifts.

▲ These figures were made to display on shelves or tables as holiday decorations.

Plants for the Holidays

Swedish children learn to appreciate nature and respect the environment at a young age. It is not surprising that grasses, tree branches, and flowers have found their way into various Swedish holiday traditions. Swedes gather birch tree branches in the spring and decorate them with feathers to represent the seasonal change of winter to spring. They celebrate midsummer by gathering garlands of flowers to decorate their homes, churches, and even their cars. They decorate a maypole with flowers, place it in the village square, and dance around it. Another Midsummer's Eve tradition requires that young people pick a variety of flowers and place the bouquets under their pillows. The legend says that if the flower-gatherers have picked enough varieties, they will dream of their future marriage partners.

Holiday *Oros*

A special *oro* often hangs over a holiday table. A smorgasbord may have hanging decorations and a gingerbread house in the middle of the table. Swedish folklore says that eating gingerbread makes people sweeter and kinder. On a special day in January, Swedish families take down their Christmas trees and happily eat the gingerbread cookies hung on the tree.

How Straw Ornaments Came to Be

Straw crafts spread from one culture to another over the centuries. In Europe, designs such as crowns, tassels, and songbirds developed as gifts. Couples exchanged them as a sign of love. Friends gave them to brides and grooms to wish them good luck. However, some researchers believe that the Swedish figures of animals and people developed for another reason.

Most Swedes' ancestors once practiced religions based on **mythology**. They believed that the gods wanted them to make offerings by giving up something valuable, such as a family member or an animal. Rather than sacrificing living things, the worshippers made straw dolls to represent people and animals. Offering the dolls let people express their good intentions without losing their loved ones and their flocks. This **ritual** ended long ago, but the straw folk art remained. The people simply adapted it for a happier use—to decorate their homes for the holidays.

Shoppers who walk into an import store near Christmastime will probably see many straw ornaments. The *jule-bucks* (Yuletide male goats) and *Tomte* (small elves or gnomes) come from Sweden.

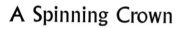

▲ *Jule-buck* ornaments decorate many homes during the holidays.

▲ This complicated *oro* was made for a very special occasion. The colored pieces are made out of felt.

A Spinning Crown

An *oro* may also hang over the dinner table at other holiday events and celebrations. At a wedding, an *oro* often hangs over the bride's place at the wedding table. It symbolizes a good harvest. Each part of the *oro* consists of short sections of straw or reed threaded onto wires or strings and joined together to make shapes. Common shapes include four-sided double pyramids and medallions. The objects are attached together to form a mobile and then decorated with feathers, ribbons, and yarn. The word *oro* means "unrest." Usually, *oros* are kept in constant motion by a nearby heat source, which is often candlelight. Candles far below the *oro* send hot air up and keep the *oro* in motion.

How to Plait, or Braid, Straw

Straw *plaiting* refers to the process of braiding or weaving hay, straw, wheat, rye, or other grass stalks. The process begins by soaking the stalks to soften them. Next, they are all cut to the same length. You can braid 2 or 3 strands, or up to 15 strands. Then the strands are sewn or laced together to create either flat or three-dimensional shapes. Geometric shapes, animal or human figures, or even baskets can be made. Swedish artisans often make goats, stars, birds, and *oros* using this method.

The straw shimmers in the light as these delicate hanging sculptures turn at the slightest breeze.

Tools

- garden clippers
- large plastic tub
- ruler

Materials

- straw; available in craft and floral stores, or collect it outdoors
- towel
- spool of 30-gauge florist's wire, available in craft and hardware stores
- scissors
- 2 sticks
- string or yarn
- feathers, shiny paper, dried flowers, or other light material

Collect the Straw

Wheat, oat, and rye are the traditional grains to use for straw craft. You can experiment with any grain that grows wild in your area. Gather straw outdoors in the summer. Look by the roadside or at parks, near fences and trees where mowers don't reach. Cut the straw close to the ground with a pair of clippers. Don't use straw from a bale, because machine-harvested straw is short and broken.

To prepare the straws, cut the grain heads off with scissors. Cut above and below each joint node, where leaves come from. Remove the leaf husks. Discard any broken or mildewed pieces. Sort the straw pieces into two piles: thick bottom pieces and thinner, more flexible top pieces. To save the straw to use later, dry it flat in the sun for a couple of days. Then store it in a dry place. *(See diagram.)*

Make the Straw Shapes

An *oro* mobile is built from a collection of individual straw shapes. Medallion and pyramid shapes are most common. Try some of each before you plan your mobile.

Medallion Shapes

1. To make a medallion, select a few of the flexible top straws. Soak them in a tub of hot water for ten minutes. Only soak as many straws as you plan to use, because leftover straw may become moldy. Bend one end of a straw to see if it has soaked long enough. If it cracks or breaks, soak it longer.

2. Cut two short pieces of stiff bottom straws, each three to four inches (7.5 to 10 cm) long. Cross them at their centers. Use scissors to cut a small piece of thin florist's wire. Wrap it around the straws in a figure eight, to hold them together. *(See diagram.)*

3. Select one of the soaked top straw pieces. Attach the end of the straw to the center of the cross by tucking it under the end of the wire. Fold the straw back on itself. *(See diagram.)*

Collect the Straw

Prepare the straw.

grain head

top piece

leaf husk

joint node

cuts

bottom pieces

Medallion Shapes

2. Cross two bottom straws.

3. Attach a soaked straw.

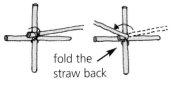

fold the straw back

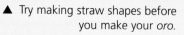
▲ Try making straw shapes before you make your *oro*.

4. Begin to wrap the straw over and around each of the four legs of the cross. Wrap in a continual outward spiral. *(See diagram.)*

5. When you reach the end of the first straw, add a new one. Slip the small end of one straw into the large end of the other. *(See diagram.)*

6. Stop when the medallion is the size you want. Put a drop of glue on the straw end, and tuck it in securely. *(See diagram.)*

Pyramid Shapes

1. To make a pyramid shape, use the thicker bottom pieces of the straw. Don't soak them. For a simple pyramid, cut three pieces of straw four inches (10 cm) long and three pieces three inches (7.5 cm) long.

2. Line the longer straws up on the table, end to end. Unroll a length of wire from the spool. Cut one piece of wire a little longer than the row of three straws. Cut three more pieces of wire, each a little longer than one of the short straws. *(See diagram.)*

3. Smooth and straighten the long piece of wire, so it will slide inside the straws without catching. Thread the three long straws onto the wire. Twist the end closed to form a triangle. This is the base of the pyramid. *(See diagram.)*

4. Thread the remaining three straws onto the three short wires. Attach each to a corner of the triangular base. Gather the tops together and twist the wire to form a pyramid. *(See Pyramid Shapes.)*

5. You can make other pyramid shapes in the same way. Duplicate the shapes illustrated here, or invent your own creative shapes.

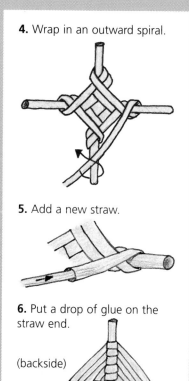
4. Wrap in an outward spiral.

5. Add a new straw.

6. Put a drop of glue on the straw end.

(backside)

glue

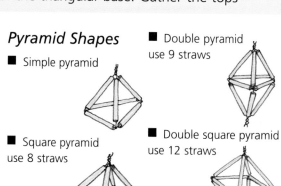
Pyramid Shapes
■ Simple pyramid
■ Double pyramid use 9 straws
■ Square pyramid use 8 straws
■ Double square pyramid use 12 straws

Pyramid Shapes
2. Cut the wire.

3. Form a triangle for the pyramid base.

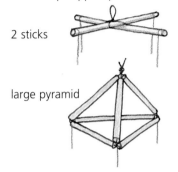

Build an *Oro* Mobile

1. The top support piece.

2 sticks

large pyramid

Oro Hints

The straw shapes can be grouped in several ways:

■ Hang small shapes inside large pyramids.

■ Hang many very small pyramids or medallions under a wide support.

■ Hang pyramids or medallions under each other in smaller and smaller sizes.

Build an *Oro* Mobile

To build a mobile, hang many straw shapes together in groups, or tiers. Then decorate the mobile with other lightweight materials. Be inventive and design a mobile that is different than any you have seen.

1. Plan your structure. The top support piece can be two crossed sticks or a very large straw pyramid. Plan the sizes of the straw shapes and how you will group them. *(See diagram and Oro Hints for ideas.)*

2. Make all the straw medallions and pyramids you need for the complete mobile. Leave medallions in a warm spot until they are completely dry. Also dry any leftover straw, if you want to save it.

3. Tie the shapes together into groups with pieces of string.

4. Make the top support. Tie a loop of string at the center, and hang it from a hook on the ceiling or the branch of a tree. Adjust it until it is balanced and hangs straight.

5. Attach the groups of straw shapes to the top support with string or yarn. Use enough string to allow the shapes to turn freely. Decorate your mobile with lightweight materials, such as yarn, shiny paper, feathers, or dried flowers.

Other Ideas

■ Make straw pyramids and medallions to hang separately as ornaments.

■ Make special ornaments to give to family and friends.

■ Use plastic or paper drinking straws to make larger shapes.

Three finished *oros* made by students.

NORWAY

SWEDEN

Storks are protected birds in Denmark. The Danes believe that they bring good luck. They often build nests on rooftops and in chimneys.

Windmills can be seen in the countryside of Northern Denmark.

The bronze statue of the Little Mermaid sits in Copenhagen harbor to celebrate Danish author Hans Christian Andersen. His fairy tales have been translated into more than 100 languages.

Skagerrak

NORTH SEA

LimFjord

Ålborg

Læsø

Kattegat Strait

Anholt

Gudená River

Jutland

Århus

Yding Skovhøj ▲

Samsø

Billund

D E N M A R K

Esbjerg

Odense

Fyn

Lake Årresø

○ Helsingør

Sjaelland

☆ **Copenhagen**

Hedebo-engen ○

Amager

Ringsted

Bornholm

BALTIC SEA

Lange-land

Lolland

N
W ✦ E
S

0   50 miles
0   75 km

At Legoland in Billund, 42 million plastic blocks have been made into scale models of a miniature city, animals, and many world-famous buildings. Children can even ride in cars made entirely of Legos.

GERMANY

POLAND

Denmark

A Jewel

As the sun rises over Denmark, Scandinavia's smallest country, some artisans begin work in their gardens. But these artisans are not gardeners in the usual sense. Instead, they copy the flowers of the countryside, along with other designs, on fabric using **embroidery,** delicately stitched needlework designs.

▲ Copenhagen is Denmark's beautiful capital. It has canals, cobblestone streets, gardens, and historic buildings.

Denmark looks small on the map, but it includes over 400 islands and the province of Greenland, or Grønland in Danish. This beautiful country is almost completely surrounded by water. Sea breezes warm the air during the winter, making the climate less harsh than the northernmost regions of Scandinavia. With no high mountains to block the wind, all of Denmark has a similar climate.

A City with Style

Copenhagen, Denmark's capital since the 15th century, is also its largest city. There are cobblestone streets and colorful old buildings with red and blue tile roofs alongside beautiful modern buildings. Tivoli Gardens, the world-famous amusement park, is located in the heart of the city. In Copenhagen, visitors can also see beautiful Danish Modern furniture, with its simple, bold design.

A City of Bicycles

Copenhagen has hundreds of cyclists. Special bike tracks both in cities and in the rural areas provide car-free roads for the many bike commuters as well as families out for a Sunday ride. Because so many people own and ride bikes regularly, Copenhagen has less traffic noise and less pollution from cars than other European capitals.

Denmark Facts

Name: Denmark (Kingdom of Denmark)
Capital: Copenhagen
Borders: Germany, Sweden, separated only by a narrow strait
Population: 5,333,617
Language: Official languages: Danish; Faeroese on the Faeroe Islands; Greenlandic (an Inuit dialect) in Greenland
Size: 16,639 sq. mi. (43,094 sq km)
High/Low Points: Yding Skovøj, 568 ft. (173 m), (Mt. Gunnbjørn in Greenland is 12,247 ft./ 3,733 m); sea level
Climate: Generally mild; average January temperature 32° F (0° C); average July temperature 62° F (17° C)
Wildlife: Red foxes, red deer, European wild rabbits, brown hares, European squirrels; Greenland has reindeer, Arctic foxes, musk oxen, polar bears, walruses, seals
Plants: Common trees include elm, beech, fir, and oak; in Greenland: mosses and lichens, polar birch, and polar willow

Greenland—Or Is It?

Greenland, the world's largest island, is part of Denmark, even though it lies 1,300 miles (2,090 km) away. About 85 percent of it lies below a permanent ice cap. Despite its name, there is little green to be seen. It was given its name by Eric the Red, a Viking who thought more people would want to go to Greenland if it had an appealing name. Today, Greenland's population is more than 58,000. Most people live near the ice-free southwest coast.

The Settling of Denmark

Denmark was shaped by **glaciers** that long ago moved their giant icy fingers over the land. There is evidence that people inhabited the land 50,000 years ago, but the last Ice Age made the region too cold for humans. About 14,000 years ago, the glaciers began to melt. The area warmed enough for nomadic tribes to return. Denmark has been settled ever since.

Shaped by Glaciers

Like other Scandinavian countries, Denmark has many lakes and streams formed by glaciers. They also formed the **fjords,** narrow inlets of the sea between steep cliffs, found along the west coast of

▲ Red deer

Jutland. There are no high mountains in Denmark. Most of the country is low, rolling land. Long ago the country was full of forests, but they were all cut down several centuries ago. This altered the environment of Denmark for all time, and as a result, many species of animals were lost. Today, the largest mammal left in Denmark is the red deer.

Access to the Sea

As far back as 5000 B.C., Denmark's many islands, harbors, and inlets provided easy access to the sea. With few natural resources to depend on, Denmark took advantage of the sea to trade for needed goods. Establishing trade routes also brought the Danes into contact with other civilizations.

Denmark has excelled in shipping and fishing since Viking times. In the early Middle Ages, many of the Vikings were Danish. The Vikings were brave but brutal sailors who raided coastal towns of Europe for 300 years. They explored many trade routes and regions in their ships made of wood from Scandinavian forests.

Bravery During World War II

Danish people strongly resisted the Nazis during World War II. King Christian X's daily horse rides through Copenhagen helped to rally the people. In 1943, the Nazis began to arrest Jews in Denmark and send them away to be killed. The Danes hid the Jews until Danish fishermen could take them by boat to Sweden and safety. About 7,000 Jews were smuggled out in this way, and the Nazis could find only about 500 to deport. The Danes sent people to visit these 500 Danish prisoners and brought food to them. The Danes caused the Nazis so much trouble that the 500 prisoners were released to Sweden, and almost all Danish Jews were saved.

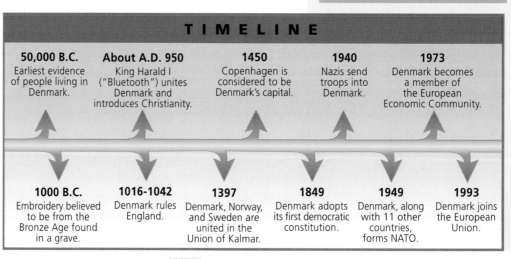

TIMELINE

50,000 B.C. Earliest evidence of people living in Denmark.	About A.D. 950 King Harald I ("Bluetooth") unites Denmark and introduces Christianity.	1450 Copenhagen is considered to be Denmark's capital.	1940 Nazis send troops into Denmark.	1973 Denmark becomes a member of the European Economic Community.
1000 B.C. Embroidery believed to be from the Bronze Age found in a grave.	**1016-1042** Denmark rules England.	**1397** Denmark, Norway, and Sweden are united in the Union of Kalmar.	**1849** Denmark adopts its first democratic constitution.	**1949** Denmark, along with 11 other countries, forms NATO.	**1993** Denmark joins the European Union.

Viking Relaxation

Danish people are fond of chess. The Vikings enjoyed board games, and one of their favorites was called *hnefatafl*. This was a game like chess but simpler. *Hnefatafl* pieces have been discovered among artifacts from the Viking period. Today, many Danes play chess, just as their Viking ancestors played *hnefatafl*.

The History of Danish Embroidery

The first Danish embroidery, a braided hair net, was found in a grave dating back to the Bronze Age (about 1,000 B.C.). The hair net belonged to a Danish noble-woman. It was made using a technique called *sprang*, which means to "braid using sticks." This find was the beginning of a rich history of Danish handcrafts.

▲ Some pieces of Danish embroidery have repeating geometric patterns.

Long ago, it was through handicrafts that Scandinavians told and passed down their stories, adventures, and history. Embroidered stories and tapestries became a way of expressing life through pictures and symbols. The oldest surviving embroidered story dates back to A.D. 800-1050. These Viking embroideries, showing images of birds, animals, and trees, were on burial clothes that were preserved in graves.

Amager Embroidery

Embroidery began to make significant changes in the 1500s, when the style of *counted thread* reached Scandinavia. Soon after, King Christian II brought Dutch farmers to Amager, an island near Copenhagen, to teach them how to grow vegetables. Through the blending of Danish and Dutch styles, Amager embroidery was formed. These designs featured imaginary animals and beasts surrounded by geometric patterns and designs.

Hedebo Embroidery

About 1760, Hedebo embroidery made its first appearance. This unique style lasted only about 100 years. Hedebo combines open work embroidery with soft curves in white. This style is very detailed. It is hard to imagine, but much of this detailed work in the past was done by candlelight. Women would sometimes place shiny objects behind a candle to reflect more light.

◄ Flowers are stitched in white in this beautiful tablecloth.

Danish Samplers

Danish embroidery design uses realistic, or lifelike, images of animals and nature. It takes serious concentration and careful mathematical counting to balance the number of lines and stitches. These skills were taught to girls at a very young age through samplers. These pieces were an important part of their education. Through samplers they would learn their names, the alphabet, and designs in cross-stitch which, like homework, would be graded. Along with spelling, girls were also taught how to make map samplers. These samplers helped to educate girls about their own country and neighboring countries. Sampler designs came from German and English pattern books. Many symbols from old samplers are still used today.

▲ In this flower sampler a Danish artisan carefully stitched the flowers of Denmark.

▲ Even embroidering a small heart takes time and patience.

Embroidery Symbols and Styles

Some symbols in Danish embroidery are universal. The unbroken circle, for example, is found in many cultures and represents wholeness and eternity. Other symbols are personal or cultural. For example, in Denmark the heart symbolizes love and the balance between intellect, spirituality, and truth. The eight-pointed star symbolizes the spirit. It has eight points, just like the points of a compass.

Denmark's culture and embroidery styles were also influenced by its association with many other countries and cultures through trading. One major trade route connected Arabia, Northern Africa, and Spain. It moved north through Western Europe and finally to Denmark.

This piece of blue ▶ embroidery was created for the edge of a pillowcase.

Gerda Bengtsson

Danish artisan Gerda Bengtsson is known for her beautiful embroidery. When she visited her sister in Rungsted, she used watercolors to paint the flowers and plants that surrounded her. When she returned home, she would embroider the gardens that she had painted.

Tools

- blunt tapestry needle, size #18, 20, or 22
- small scissors
- pencil

Materials

- cross-stitch fabric such as cotton Aida cloth, with a count of 7, 8, or 11; available in needlepoint or craft stores
- 6-strand cotton embroidery floss in many colors
- paper
- graph paper with 1/8-in. (3 mm) squares; available at stationery stores
- masking tape
- sewing thread
- picture frame, mat, and backing
- white craft glue

Experiment with Cross-Stitch

1. Cross-stitch fabric.

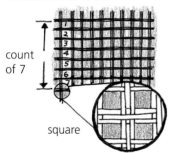

count of 7

square

6. End a row of cross-stitch.

Cross-stitching is easy to do. First, practice the stitches, and then make a sampler to show what you have learned.

Experiment with Cross-Stitch

Cross-stitch is a Danish favorite. To make a cross-stitch sampler, you will work from a graph paper pattern. You'll count the threads of the cloth and sew in the spaces between them. Practice the cross-stitch and the other stitches shown on page 24 before you plan your sampler.

1. Choose a fabric. Special cross-stitch fabrics such as Aida cloth are woven with several threads grouped together. These are easier to use for cross-stitch than regular fabric. If you are a beginner, choose a cloth with a count of seven. This means that it has seven holes per inch (2.5 cm). Each stitch will cover one group of threads, called a square. *(See diagram.)*

2. Cut a small piece of cross-stitch fabric to use for a test.

3. Choose a tapestry needle that fits easily through the spaces of your cloth. Cut a one-foot (30-cm) piece of six-strand embroidery floss. Divide it into two 3-strand pieces. Thread a needle with one piece. Don't tie a knot.

4. Start a row of cross-stitch.

4. Sit in a comfortable position and use good light to prevent eye strain. Relax and enjoy yourself! Start by sewing up from the back side of the fabric to the front. Leave a short tail of thread in the back. Hold the tail flat to the back and catch it under the first stitches. *(See diagram.)*

5. Sew one row of each of the stitches. Pull the stitches tight enough to make a smooth stitch, but not so tight that the cloth forms wrinkles.

6. To end a row of stitches, weave back under a few stitches on the back side of the work. Clip the thread. *(See diagram.)*

Sew one row of each of the ▶ stitches shown on page 24.

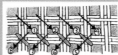

Plan a Sampler

Look through cross-stitch pattern books to get ideas for your sampler. You can copy a pattern from a book, but it's more fun to create your own.

1. Decide on the subject of your sampler and make a small sketch. Hearts, snowflakes, flowers, people, and animals are all commonly used as sampler designs or borders.

2. Traditional samplers also contain the alphabet. Instead of the whole alphabet, you might stitch a short phrase or the name of your pet, as in the samplers shown on page 25. Choose a cross-stitch alphabet that you like from a book listed in the Resources on page 46 or from another pattern book.

Stitches You Will Use

cross-stitch – Make a row of diagonal stitches over one square each. Then stitch back in the other direction, crossing the first stitches. Or sew individual cross-stitches one at a time.

braided cross-stitch – Make one regular cross-stitch, ending in the bottom left. Then take a long diagonal stitch from the top left. Stitch over the cross-stitch and end in the space to the right. Cross back with a short stitch, then repeat the long stitch.

running stitch – Sew in and out of the spaces in any direction.

backstitch – Sew backwards over one square, then forward under two squares. Repeat.

cross-stitch

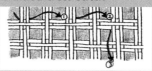
braided cross-stitch

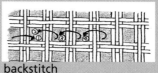
running stitch

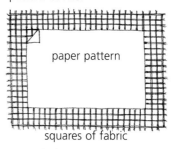
backstitch

Plan a Sampler

3. Cut paper to the size of your sampler.

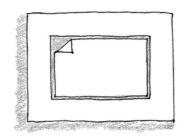

3. Cut a piece of paper to the size and shape you want for your finished sampler. If you know the size of your picture frame, you can use those measurements. *(See diagram.)*

4. Hold the paper pattern on the cross-stitch fabric. Count how many squares of fabric the pattern covers, in both directions. This tells how many stitches you can make. *(See diagram.)*

5. Now count out and mark the same number of squares on a piece of graph paper. Each square on the graph is equal to one square on the cross-stitch fabric. Mark the vertical and horizontal center lines. *(See diagram.)*

6. Draw the sampler design and border on the graph paper. Make sure the design is centered. Draw around the edges of the graph squares. Count and mark how many squares you need for the letters you want to stitch. *(See diagram.)*

4. Count the squares the pattern covers.

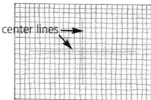
paper pattern

squares of fabric

5. Mark the measurements on the graph paper.

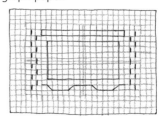
center lines

6. Draw a sampler design on graph paper.

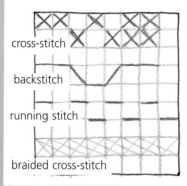

7. Label the different stitches.

cross-stitch

backstitch

running stitch

braided cross-stitch

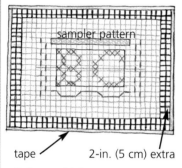

Stitch a Sampler

1. Cut the fabric.

sampler pattern

tape

2-in. (5 cm) extra

2. Sew guidelines.

letter guideline

center lines

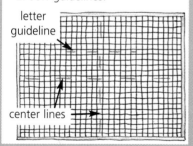

Other Ideas

■ Make your sampler into a pillow. Cut a backing of cotton fabric the same size as your sampler. Pin the two pieces with good sides together. Sew and fill with fiberfill.

7. Label the different stitches. Mark each cross-stitch with an X. The backstitch and running stitch are often used for outlines, stems, borders, and details. Mark them as dotted lines. The braided cross-stitch is also used for borders and for filling large areas. *(See diagram.)*

8. Choose the thread colors you will use. Use colored pencils to mark the graph with the thread colors.

Stitch a Sampler

1. Cut the cross-stitch fabric to the size of your sampler, plus two inches (5 cm) extra on each side. If the cloth begins to fray, or unravel, wrap the edges with masking tape. *(See diagram.)*

2. Fold the fabric in half by its width and in half again by its height to find the vertical and horizontal centers. With plain sewing thread, sew with long running stitches along both centers as temporary guidelines. You can also sew a guideline for the bottom of a row of letters. *(See diagram.)*

3. Now, begin to cross-stitch! Decide on the best place to start. Sometimes it's best to work from the bottom of a design to the top. Sometimes it's better to work outward from the center. Whichever you choose, count from the center lines, not the outside edge. Stitch all of the cross-stitches first, then add the outlining stitches and details.

4. When you are finished stitching your sampler, carefully remove the masking tape from the edges. Clip and pull out the temporary guide threads. To remove wrinkles, iron the sampler face down on a thick towel.

5. To frame your sampler, cut a piece of heavy backing board the same size as the picture mat. Center the sampler on the board and glue the edges down with white craft glue. When the glue is dry, put the mat on top of the sampler. Frame with or without glass.

▲ Students stitched these samplers with the names and pictures of their pets and other favorite words.

ARCTIC OCEAN

Nordaustlandet

Edgeøya

Svalbard

BARENTS
SEA

A reindeer herder near Karasjok
feeds two of her animals on a
snowfield.

The Arctic fox lives in treeless
Arctic regions and in islands in
the Arctic Ocean. Its fur changes
from brown or gray to pure white
in winter.

Bjørnøya

NORWEGIAN
SEA

North Cape
(Nordkapp)

Hammerfest

Karasjok

Lake
Inari

Jaeggevarre

Kautokeino

Murmansk

NORWAY

Inari

Lake
Imandra

Lake
Torne

L A P L A N D

Mt.
Kebnekaise

Kiruna

Kirovsk

Kola
Peninsula

Svartisen

Jukkasjärvi

Rovaniemi

Jokkmokk

Arctic Circle

Kemi River

WHITE
SEA

SWEDEN

RUSSIA

A Saami fisherman checks his
nets that are drying on the shore
of a lake near Jukkasjarvi.

FINLAND

Skateboarders in downtown
Kiruna enjoy the spring weather.

GULF OF
BOTHNIA

N
W   E
S

0   100 miles
0   150 km

Gulf of
Finland

BALTIC
SEA

ESTONIA

Lapland

▲ Above the Arctic Circle the sun does not set from about mid-May until the end of July.

Lapland Facts

Name: Lapland—the area north of the Arctic Circle that includes part of Norway, Sweden, Finland, and a small part of Russia
Population: about 113,000
Language: Finno-Ugrian (closely related to Finnish) with many dialects; many Saami also speak the language of their neighbors
Size: About 150,000 sq. mi. (388,000 sq km)
Climate: Very cold, with winter for eight to nine months of every year; the other months are much like spring; winter temperatures can reach lows of -58° F (-50° C)
Wildlife: Reindeer, arctic fox, lynx, and wolverines; many species of birds, including three-toed woodpeckers and golden eagles; Atlantic salmon, brown trout
Plants: Lichens, mosses; miniature varieties of birch, spruce, pine, and fir trees; small mountain wildflowers; berries, including the cloudberry, cranberry, and blueberry

Official Crossing

Rovaniemi, Finland, is known as the "center" of Lapland. The city dates back 8,000 years, but the original town was destroyed by the Nazis in 1944. Architect Alvar Aalto designed a new modern town with roads shaped like reindeer antlers! Rovaniemi is located right on the Arctic Circle. From here, tourists cross the Arctic Circle and receive a certificate to bring home as a souvenir.

North of the Arctic Circle

Lapland is a region above the Arctic Circle that includes the northernmost parts of Norway, Sweden, Finland, and the Kola Peninsula area of Russia. It is not a separate country. Lapland usually brings up images of a very cold place somewhere near the North Pole where there are many reindeer. This picture is only part of the rich history and traditions of the region and the Saami people who have lived there for thousands of years.

Darkness and Light

Lapland is called "the land of eight seasons," but in fact, many parts of Lapland seem to have just two. Lapland winters leave the region frozen and white for nine months of every year. The other three months resemble spring. The Arctic Circle marks the edge of an area where the sun never rises for a period of several months each winter. The "midnight sun" refers to the period from about mid-May until the end of July, when the sun never sets. Imagine how it must feel to see the sun after months of dark, wintry weather. Even today, the return of the sun brings great celebration!

It is no surprise that the Saami of long ago worshiped the sun and many other nature gods. Sun god symbols were often painted on the heads of their magic drums. These magic drums once played a major role in the everyday life of the Saami people.

Aurora Borealis, or Northern Lights

The northern lights appear in the night sky of the far northern regions of the Earth. These brilliant light displays appear as playful flickers or streaks of green, red, and purple lights. They may stretch across the sky for thousands of miles.

▲ In the late 1800s Saami people dressed in thick fur coats.

"Europe's Most Primitive and Distinctive People"

It is unknown exactly when and from where the Saami people came to Lapland. Some researchers believe they may have come from Asia thousands of years ago.

The Saami have been described as "Europe's most primitive and distinctive people." However, it is important not to confuse "primitive" with unintelligent or unworthy of respect. Many of the first people to come upon the Saami made that mistake. Early reports described a strange race of people where women hunted alongside men and took their share of the kill. Other stories described a small, dark-haired, gnome-like people who dressed in animal skins, burrowed underground for the winter, or who lived high in the trees. They were said to jump around on wooden shoes rather than walking and to slide along the ground like snakes. The stories grew until the Saami people did not seem human.

In truth, the Saami are among the smallest people in Europe. The men are about 5 feet tall (150 cm), the women about four inches (10 cm) shorter. At times they did construct shelters that were partly underground in order to hold the heat better. They wore animal skin coats for warmth, stored meat in treetops to protect it from hungry wolves, and carried their houses with them. They invented a way to move quickly across the snow and ice on large skis, using sticks to control their movements. The Saami were known for their great ability to run on skis.

Laws Prohibit Saami Beliefs

Many of the region's first visitors were critical of the Saami people's belief in the supernatural and in many unseen gods. The Saami believed that spirits lived in animals, mountains, water, and rocks. When missionaries arrived in the 17th century, they wanted to convert the Saami people to Christianity and a belief in one God. Saami spiritual beliefs were outlawed. A law was passed requiring Saami people to go to church. They were told to burn or bury their magic drums and other religious symbols. The old songs were forbidden, along with traditional celebrations and games. The failure to obey sometimes resulted in death.

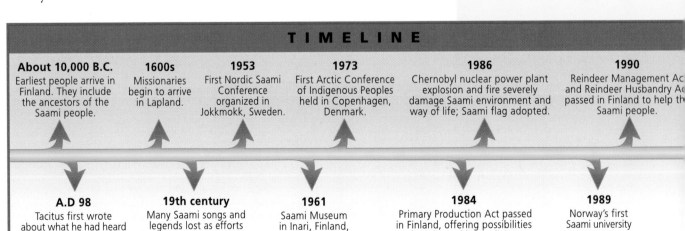

T I M E L I N E

About 10,000 B.C.
Earliest people arrive in Finland. They include the ancestors of the Saami people.

1600s
Missionaries begin to arrive in Lapland.

1953
First Nordic Saami Conference organized in Jokkmokk, Sweden.

1973
First Arctic Conference of Indigenous Peoples held in Copenhagen, Denmark.

1986
Chernobyl nuclear power plant explosion and fire severely damage Saami environment and way of life; Saami flag adopted.

1990
Reindeer Management Ac and Reindeer Husbandry A passed in Finland to help th Saami people.

A.D 98
Tacitus first wrote about what he had heard about the Fenni, an early name for the Saami.

19th century
Many Saami songs and legends lost as efforts increase to stamp out the old Saami way of life.

1961
Saami Museum in Inari, Finland, completed.

1984
Primary Production Act passed in Finland, offering possibilities for jobs and better living conditions for the Saami in Finland.

1989
Norway's first Saami university opens.

A Chilly But Diverse Environment

The far north is not a friendly environment for people or animals. The temperature can dip down to a chilly -58° F (-50° C). The wind is so fierce that it can sink small boats in lakes. It uproots huge forest trees and makes mountain birch trees bend over and cower as they brush the ground.

Lapland is a cold, harsh environment, but it is not all snow and ice. The frozen **tundra** of northern Norway contrasts with the deep fjords, or narrow inlets, between the steep slopes of the coast. Lapland has forests, lakes, mountain chains, and lowland areas. As a nomadic people, the Saami followed reindeer herds in their yearly migration, or movement, from winter forest lands to their summer grazing grounds in higher pastures.

Long ago, the Saami people depended on reindeer for meat, milk, clothing, hides for tents, and as pack animals. Reindeer were vital to the Saami, and reindeer symbols appeared often on magic drums. Many Saami still make a living raising reindeer, but only a small percentage still lead the nomadic life of their ancestors. Reindeer herders today use helicopters, snowmobiles, and walkie-talkies to help them. Some Saami make a living by fishing or farming. Others work in offices, stores, or other businesses in the cities.

Living on Nature's Terms

The Saami people knew how to work with nature on its own terms. Although times have changed, they still treat the environment with great respect. Natural resources, such as berry bushes, reindeer pastures, farmland, hunting grounds, mushrooms, and water are all important to Saami economy. They make sure their activities do not strain the environment's ability to provide for their needs, adapting their fishing and hunting if necessary to support the environment.

Chernobyl— A True Disaster

In 1986, a fire and explosion at the Chernobyl Nuclear Plant, located near Kiev, Ukraine, had devastating effects on the Saami people. In Lapland, the fallout from this explosion poisoned the lichen that the reindeer eat. Game, fish, berries, and fungi were also contaminated. People could not depend on the land for survival in the way they had before. As a result, traditional Saami arts and crafts began to gain importance as a means of income.

A Really Cool Hotel!

The Saami people know how to withstand icy cold weather. Today, tourists can test their endurance by reserving a room in an ice hotel that is rebuilt every winter near Jukkasjarvi, Sweden. Ten thousand tons of ice are used to create a 29-room hotel. Guests are issued thermal jumpsuits to help withstand below-freezing temperatures. Beds are blocks of ice covered with reindeer skins. For sleeping comfort, people are given insulated body bags like those used by astronauts. The hotel is open each year until it begins to thaw!

Saami Oral Tradition

Oral tradition managed to preserve many ancient beliefs lost after the introduction of Christianity. The oldest Saami stories date back to "the time when light was made." Some stories talk about historic events for which no other information exists. Many stories are of the Wind Man, a being who could unleash fierce winds at will. The wind god was an important symbol represented on many magic drums.

The Wind Man

According to Saami myth, Biegolmai, the Wind Man, had two giant shovels. With them he would scoop up the snow and wind and dump them both with great force on Lapland. But one time, during a big snowstorm, one of Biegolmai's shovels broke. The wind died down. It was only then that a few plants could timidly take hold.

Saami Languages

The Saami often claim up to seven languages. They reflect the importance of nature, the weather, seasons, and reindeer to the Saami people. Their languages have affected neighboring languages. For example, expressions associated with nature, hunting, and reindeer have become a part of the Finnish spoken in northern Finland.

Today, the Saami people often speak the language of their neighbors, and many Saami are **bilingual**. Saami language courses are now taught in many Scandinavian schools, and courses in other subjects are taught in the Saami language. Saami radio stations, magazines, and newspapers also help to preserve the language.

Yoiking

Yoiking (yoy-IK-ing) is an unusual type of singing that sounds like a type of yodeling. Saami people use *yoiks* to comment on important events. *Yoiks* may be about nature, animals, or people. Sometimes *yoiks* imitate animals like the wolf, reindeer, and duck. Long ago, *yoiks* were a part of **rituals**. Today, *yoiking* can be a part of a ceremony or social event. Folk music from Lapland is currently part of the world music scene. Some popular bands combine folk, rock, jazz—and *yoiking*.

No Word for War

The Saami language contains over 90 words to describe different snow conditions. There are words for eight seasons. It is said that about one-fourth of the words in the central Saami dialect are related to reindeer. The Saami language, however, has no word for strange concepts like war.

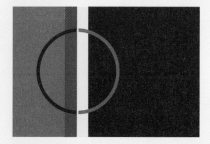

Saami Flag

The Saami flag is one way the Saami people honor their history. The idea for the flag was taken from the magic drums. The red and blue circles are symbols of the sun and moon. The colors in the flag—red, blue, yellow, and green—are those used in traditional Saami costumes.

"Great Winter Market"

Jokkmokk, Sweden, is an important center of Saami culture and tradition. In February a big market is held, where visitors can see the handicrafts made by the Saami people. The Saami usually dress in brightly colored costumes for the festival. At the Great Winter Market, tourists can also sample Saami foods, such as reindeer and moose salami.

Saami Dress

Traditional Saami costumes are themselves works of art, with their bright, multicolored ribbon, braid, or beadwork trim around the neck, shoulders, and wrists. Red, blue, green, and yellow are the colors used most often. Perhaps the Saami made these colorful garments to stand out against the stark white background of snow and ice.

Hats of the Four Winds

The costumes in each region differ, and this includes the hats. Saami men in Norway traditionally wear "hats of the four winds." These hats have four points, like a jester's hat. In some areas, Saami women wear hats with flaps to protect their ears against the cold wind. In Sweden, traditional Saami hats have large red pompoms.

A Revival of Saami Arts

A recent revival of Saami traditions and pride in their ancestry has focused attention on Saami arts. The outdoor Lapp Museum in Inari, Finland, is a good example. Inari is an important center of Saami culture. There, tourists can see Saami buildings and artifacts that have been either preserved or rebuilt.

In places like Inari and Jokkmokk, many Saami items of clothing, such as reindeer slippers and purses, brightly colored hats, and woven belts, are now sold to tourists. The Saami also make beautiful objects carved from bone and wood. Many of them are decorated with ancient symbols once seen on magic drums.

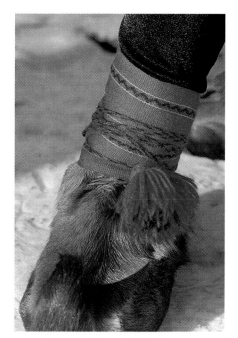

Traditional Saami ▶ shoes are made out of reindeer fur.

Magic Drums

Long ago, only shamans had the special powers to communicate with the gods, demons, and the spirits of Saami ancestors. The shamans used their magical powers to cure people who were ill, control events, and make predictions. The shamans sometimes used magic drums to communicate with the gods. Images of people, animals, dwellings, gods, nature, and Saami daily life were drawn on the heads of the magic drums. The sun and wind were especially meaningful to the Saami, and these images often appeared on the drums.

Beating the Drum

Anyone could own a magic drum, but only shamans could use a drum to communicate with the spirits, cure the sick, or predict the future. Shamans could predict the time of the next hunt, the harshness of the coming winter, the tribe's health, or the success of the next fishing season.

To do this, the shaman would beat the oval drum using a small stick with a handle made from reindeer horn. Small pieces of wood or rings were placed on the drawing of the sun on the tightly stretched drum head. When the drum was beaten, the objects bounced around onto the other images painted on the drum. When the shaman stopped drumming, he would interpret the meaning of each object's final resting place.

The Saami People Today

Like many other indigenous, or native, people around the world, the Saami were treated badly by those who did not share their beliefs. Over the centuries, many of the old Saami traditions, beliefs, and stories were lost. However, today many Saami people are working to preserve their language and traditions. The paintings on Saami drums are important reminders of the time when the Saami people moved quietly over Lapland in peaceful harmony with the plants, animals, and seasons.

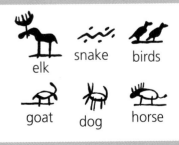

◀ This Saami drum, made from reindeer leather, is covered with painted symbols.

▲ The doors to Kiruna Stadshus, the Kiruna town hall, have Saami magic drum handles made of reindeer horn and birch wood.

Saami Drum Images

■ Forces of nature

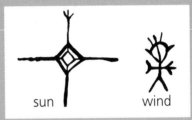

sun   wind

■ Everyday life

reindeer corral   snow sleigh   storehouse

■ Animals

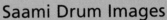

elk   snake   birds

goat   dog   horse

32

Tools

- wood file
- bathtub or plastic pool
- 2 bricks or other weights
- strong nylon rope or cord, 8 ft. (2.5 m) long
- 2 C-clamps
- ruler
- hammer
- scissors
- pliers

Materials

- piece of 1/4-in. (5 mm) plywood, 4 ft. by 4 in. (1 m by 10 cm)
- wood glue
- nails, 1/2-in. (12 mm) and 1-in. (2.5 cm)
- 3-ft. (1 m) long piece of 1- by 2-in. (2.5 by 5 cm) lumber
- varnish
- rawhide; cow, goat, or deer, from a leather supply store
- transfer paper
- acrylic paint
- Y-shaped stick
- fur or yarn
- ring of wood or plastic

5. Overlap the ends.

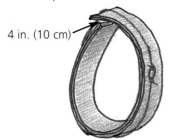

4 in. (10 cm)

Making a drum isn't difficult, but it does take time. It's fun to build one together with friends.

Make the Drum Frame

Many Saami drums are frame drums, made with a round strip of wood bent into an oval. Sometimes it is possible to buy drum frames, ready to stretch. If you want to make your own, try this simple plywood frame. The plywood must be bent very slowly or it will crack. The whole bending process may take two or three days.

1. Ask an adult to cut the plywood into a strip four feet long by four inches wide (1 m by 10 cm). Cut it so the grain of the wood runs in the narrow direction as shown. File the edges smooth. *(See diagram.)*

2. Fill a bathtub or plastic pool with water. Place the plywood strip flat on the bottom. Weight it in the center with a brick to keep it underwater. Let it soak for several hours. The plywood will begin to bow into an arc.

3. Tie a small loop in one end of a long piece of cord or rope. Turn the plywood strip on its edge, and wrap the cord around the outside. Insert the loose end of cord through the loop, and pull it just until the cord is rigid. Tie the loose end to hold the strip in this shallow arc shape. *(See diagram.)*

Make the Drum Frame

1. Cut the plywood strip.

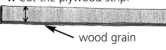

wood grain

4 ft. (1 m) by 4 in. (10 cm)

3. Wrap a cord around the strip.

4. The ends meet.

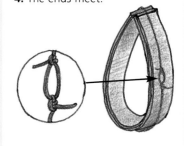

4. Soak the wood again. Every two to four hours, tighten the cord a little more. Pull the ends of the strip an inch or two (2.5 to 5 cm) closer together. Continue until the ends meet, and the strip is teardrop-shaped. *(See diagram.)*

5. Now, lap one end of the strip over the other by four inches (10 cm). Gently press and round the ends with your hands. Begin to make gentle changes to shape your drum frame. Remember to work slowly! If you force the wood, it will crack. Retie the cord and soak the wood again. *(See diagram.)*

6. When the overlapped ends are softened, loosely attach two C-clamps and soak the wood. Tighten the clamps little by little until the overlap is rounded and smooth. *(See diagram.)*

7. Remove the plywood from the water, and allow it to dry thoroughly. Remove the clamps.

8. File the outside narrow edge to a slant. Glue the overlapped ends with carpenter's glue. Tack along both the inside and outside edges of the overlap with three 1/2-inch (12 mm) nails. Clamp the overlap again, and dry the glue overnight. *(See diagram.)*

9. Measure the length and width of the inside of your drum frame. Cut two crossbars from one- by two-inch (2.5 by 5 cm) lumber. Cut them long enough to fit snugly inside the frame. Dab glue on the ends. Slide the first crosspiece in so that it is flush with the bottom edge of the frame. Rest the second crosspiece on the first, leaving a space at the top. Tack each end with a one-inch (2.5 cm) nail. *(See diagram.)*

10. Seal the plywood with varnish, inside and out. The drum frame is ready!

Stretch the Drum Head

1. Choose a piece of rawhide for your drum. Cow hide is thick and will produce a drum with a low sound. Goat hide is thinner and will have a higher tone. Deer hide is in-between.

2. Draw a rough circle on the rawhide, three to five inches (7.5 to 12.5 cm) bigger than the frame. Mark the lacing holes with a pencil. Make an even number of dots 1/2-inch (12 mm) in from the edge of the circle and about two inches (about 5 cm) apart. *(See diagram.)*

3. Soak the rawhide in cool water for at least one hour until it is soft. Lay the wet hide on a towel. Use sharp scissors to cut around the circle. Pinch the hide and cut a small V for each lacing hole.

4. Now measure to find the thong length. Put the frame on the circle of hide, and measure from one hole to the opposite hole. Add an extra five inches (12.5 cm) on each side for tying. Put the circle of hide back in water so it will stay soft. *(See diagram.)*

◀ Friends can help you stretch the drum head.

6. Attach the C-clamps.

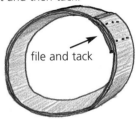

8. File the narrow edge to a slant and then tack.

file and tack

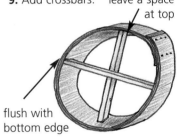

9. Add crossbars.   leave a space at top

flush with bottom edge

Stretch the Drum Head

2. Draw a circle.

2 in. (5 cm) apart

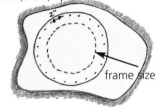

frame size

4. Measure the thong length.

add 5 in. (12.5 cm)

5. Cut the thongs.

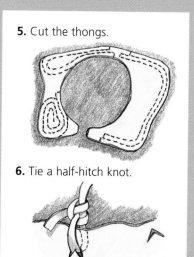

6. Tie a half-hitch knot.

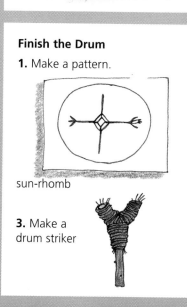

Finish the Drum

1. Make a pattern.

sun-rhomb

3. Make a
drum striker

5. Cut lacing thongs 1/2-inch (12 mm) wide from the leftover hide. Look at the illustration for ways to cut long thongs from scraps of hide. Cut half as many thongs as the number of holes. Put the thongs back in water as you cut them, so they will stay soft. *(See diagram.)*

6. Now you are ready to stretch the drum head! Spread the hide circle back out on the towel. Center the frame on top of it. Thread one thong through a hole and tie a half-hitch knot. Stretch the thong straight across to the opposite hole. Thread the thong and pull it as tight as you can. Use pliers to get a grip on the slippery thong, and pull hard. Tie a knot on that side, also. *(See diagram.)*

7. Continue until all the holes are threaded and tied. Let the drum dry for two days. The hide will tighten more as it dries and shrinks.

Finish the Drum

The beautiful little pictures on the Saami drums are delightful. They are simple, but lively. Decide what pictures to paint on your drum. Include symbols of your life, things you like to do, and your hopes for the future. Study the images on page 32 for ideas.

1. Trace around your drum on paper to make a pattern. Draw your pictures. Many Saami drums have a central design called a sun-rhomb—a diamond with four rays. Other designs are painted around the edges of the drum. *(See diagram.)*

2. Transfer the pattern to the hide with transfer paper. Paint the designs with acrylic paint. Traditionally the pictures are a reddish-brown color.

3. Make a drum striker from a slender T- or Y-shaped tree branch. Cut it with a pruner, then file and sand it smooth. Wrap the top of the striker with a strip of fur, cloth, or yarn. Also, find a wooden or plastic ring or bracelet to use for making predictions. Tie it to the drum with a long piece of yarn. *(See diagram.)*

4. The Saami people tune their drums in front of a campfire. The heat tightens up the hide and improves the sound of the drum. If you live in a damp climate, tune the drum with a hair dryer. If you live in a hot, dry climate, moisten the drum with water.

5. Your drum is ready to play! Place the ring on the drum. Beat the drum, and watch as the ring bounces and moves over the pictures. Have fun using the drum to tell a story or make predictions.

NORWEGIAN SEA

Atlantic puffins perch on rocks on the coast of the Barents Sea.

BARENTS SEA

North Cape (Nordkapp)

Fjords are found along Norway's rugged coastline. They were formed over one million years ago.

Tromsø

And Fjord

Lofoten Islands

Vest Fjord

FINLAND

Svartisen Glacier ◆

- - - A r c t i c   C i r c l e - - -

Trondheim Fjord

Trondheim ○

SWEDEN

NORWAY

Galdhøpiggen ▲

Glåma River

Lillehammer ○

Gulf of Bothnia

Traditional Norwegian folk dancing is performed during Oslo's summer folk festivals.

Sogne Fjord

Hardanger Plateau

Bergen ○

Oslo ★

Bokn Fjord **Telemark Region**

Drammen ○

Stavanger ○

Kristiansand ○

Skagerrak

Gulf of Finland

ESTONIA

RUSSIA

Gulf of Riga

LATVIA

Kattegat Strait

Beautiful Viking ships are on display at the Viking Ship Museum in Oslo. The Vikings buried their chiefs in these ships.

BALTIC SEA

NORTH SEA

D E N M A R K

LITHUANIA

RUSSIA

N
W · E
S

GERMANY

POLAND

| 0 | | 200 miles |
| 0 | | 300 km |

Norway

Norway is a long, narrow country on the northwest edge of the European continent. It extends farther north than any other European country. Oslo, Norway's historic capital, is located in the southern end of the country. It lies at the end of a long fjord, a narrow inlet that cuts into the mountains that surround the city.

▲ Oslo, Norway's capital, lies at the end of a long fjord.

Norway Facts

Name: Norway (Kingdom of Norway); the name comes from *Nordweg,* or "way to the north"
Capital: Oslo
Borders: Sweden, Finland, Russia
Population: 4,446,000
Language: Norwegian (official); many dialects
Size: 125,052 sq. mi. (323,883 sq km)
High/Low Points: Galdhøpiggen, 8,100 ft. (2,469 m) above sea level; sea level along the coast
Climate: Generally milder than other far north regions, especially in the lowlands; higher inland regions much colder; temp. ranges from a high of 64° F (18° C) in July to a low of 10° F (-12° C) in January; far north has continuous daylight from mid-May through July
Wildlife: Red deer; wolverines, reindeer, and other Arctic animals; Atlantic puffins, lemmings, kittiwakes, white snowy owls, sea eagles; brown trout, Atlantic salmon, gray seals, minke whales, sei whales, gray whales
Plants: About 2,000 species of plants; mosses, lichens, and bog-cotton grass; rose-tinted heaths and species of Arctic plants; wild berries, including cloudberries, a species of the rose family little known outside the region; thick spruce and pine forests

A Glimpse of the Past

Today, visitors can glimpse Norway's rich history in Oslo's open-air Folk Museum. At the museum, old historic farm buildings, houses, and churches from different parts of Norway are on display. A short distance away, some of Norway's greatest treasures—Viking ships dating from the ninth century—are preserved. And at the Kon-Tiki Museum, visitors can see the original raft on which the famous Norwegian scientist Thor Heyerdahl and his five companions drifted across the Pacific Ocean for over 5,000 miles (8047 km) in 1947.

"The Land of the Midnight Sun"

The northern part of Norway that lies above the Arctic Circle is called "The Land of the Midnight Sun." Here, the sun does not set during the summer. Even below the Arctic Circle, it is so light that people can read outdoors in the middle of the night by natural light. They think nothing of taking a walk to visit friends at 3:00 A.M.! But there are also several months of darkness. People who live north of the Arctic Circle do not see the sun for many weeks in winter, although there is a slight brightness around the middle of the day.

Dark Winter Nights

Some say that *rosemaling,* a special style of Norwegian folk art painting, began because farmers needed something to do during the long, dark winter nights. They chose colors and designs that were like the bright flowers that appeared only after the sun returned in the summertime.

Here Comes the Sun!

When the sun returns in late January, after two months of continual darkness, it's time to celebrate. Some children in northern Norway get the day off from school to watch for its arrival. They can't be late. On the first day, the sun peeks above the horizon for just four minutes.

Norway's Geography

Norway is a very mountainous country—a high, rugged **plateau** of bare rock smoothed long ago by ancient glaciers. Like a craggy backbone, mountain ranges run almost the full length of the country. Some of these mountains are so steep that no one has ever dared to climb them. Many Norwegians used the mountains as hiding places from the Germans during World War II.

▲ Norway's mountains have played an important part in the country's history.

Much of the plateau is covered with snow, broken only by hundreds of narrow fjords that bring the sea inland. The fjords were created during the Ice Age, over one million years ago.

The Viking Age

The Vikings were an important part of Scandinavian history. They lived in what is now Norway, Sweden, and Denmark from about A.D. 800 to 1100. Most Vikings lived peacefully in well-organized settlements. But the Vikings were best known as fierce pirates and warriors. They terrorized Western Europe for about 300 years as they conquered areas in England, Scotland, and Ireland.

The Vikings were daring sailors who explored uncharted waters in their sleek dragonhead ships. They searched for new trade routes while they conquered new territories. The Vikings landed on the coast of North America 500 years before Columbus arrived in 1492. They built beautiful wooden ships and were among the best ship-builders of their time.

Norway Takes a Stand

Norway has one of the highest standards of living in the world. The country is also famous for its bold stands on social issues. For example, violence of any kind, even among cartoon characters, is closely monitored.

Raven Navigation

The Vikings are said to have sometimes used ravens to help them when sailing on uncharted oceans. They knew that ravens flew toward land, so they would release a raven from the ship and watch which way it flew. Then they would sail in the same direction.

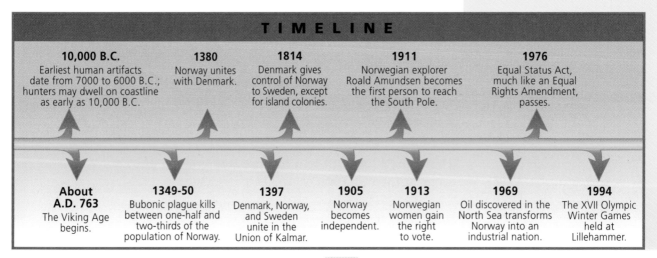

TIMELINE

10,000 B.C. Earliest human artifacts date from 7000 to 6000 B.C.; hunters may dwell on coastline as early as 10,000 B.C.	**1380** Norway unites with Denmark.	**1814** Denmark gives control of Norway to Sweden, except for island colonies.	**1911** Norwegian explorer Roald Amundsen becomes the first person to reach the South Pole.	**1976** Equal Status Act, much like an Equal Rights Amendment, passes.

About A.D. 763 The Viking Age begins.	**1349-50** Bubonic plague kills between one-half and two-thirds of the population of Norway.	**1397** Denmark, Norway, and Sweden unite in the Union of Kalmar.	**1905** Norway becomes independent.	**1913** Norwegian women gain the right to vote.	**1969** Oil discovered in the North Sea transforms Norway into an industrial nation.	**1994** The XVII Olympic Winter Games held at Lillehammer.

▲ This Danish house proudly displays shutters with rosemaling.

Trunks

Norwegians who came to the United States needed something in which to carry their possessions. Trunks were commonly used. They also provided a reason for rosemaling. In addition to a design, the person's name and the year were usually added to it. The fanciest trunks were dowry trunks. Young women prepared for marriage by storing treasures they were making for their own homes in these trunks.

Many trunks were lost at sea during the voyage to the United States. Some were also damaged or lost during the journey across the country to the Midwest. However, those that survived have been passed down in families or are on display in museums.

Farmers as Painters

Rosemaling started on farms in the Telemark region of Norway in the mid-1700s. It slowly made its way over the mountains to the west coast. As farmers acquired their own land, they had a purpose for creating art. Whether they painted small, practical objects or an entire wall of their house, it gave them a sense of pride. They were painting something they owned, something they could pass down from generation to generation.

Painting on the Walls

Norwegian houses were cozy but dreary places to be during the long, dark winter months. Because there were very few glass windows, colorful tapestries were hung on the thick log walls to brighten up the room.

Fireplaces were in the center of the room, with a smoke hole in the roof to allow smoke to escape. As more glass windows were added over time, houses had more light. People could see how dirty the walls were from years of smoke. They began to paint the walls, which provided a base coat for rosemaling.

Rosemaling Moves West

By the early 1800s, there were too many rosemalers in eastern Norway. Artisans had to travel across the mountains to western Norway, where rosemaling was less well-known, to make a living. Imagine painters heading over the mountains with their paints in a sack on their backs. In winter they simply skied over the mountains! Some painters painted boxes and other items. Other painters were hired to paint churches.

Over the Seas

By the 1850s, rosemaling was on the decline. Many poor farmers and artisans, tempted by promises of a better life, left Norway in the last half of the 19th century. They **emigrated**, or left their own land and country, to travel to the United States to live. Many of them settled in parts of the Midwest, including Minnesota, Wisconsin, and Iowa. Leaving their homeland and arriving in a new country provided a new purpose for rosemaling once again.

Rosemaling Designs

In the old days, rosemaling designs were very individual. People knew who painted a piece without even seeing the signature. It was said that it was even possible to tell the mood the painter was in at the time!

▲ Imagine packing a sandwich in this beautiful Norwegian lunch box!

Styles also tended to represent the character of a particular area. Telemark designs, for example, were very creative. Telemark painters did not copy patterns or forms from the past. Often, they combined C and S curves to create pleasing designs. Gold leaf was sometimes added as well.

When scrolls, leaves, and flowers were combined in a pleasing pattern, it was said to be a good rosemaling design. Round designs were particularly hard to paint, so a compass was—and still is— often used to help plan the painting.

Storytelling Designs

Some rosemaling designs tell a story. They may relate stories from the Bible. Other designs tell about a famous person or document an important event, like a wedding. Lettering and sayings were also popular additions to rosemaling designs. Dowry chests included the name of the bride and her family. Poetry, sayings, or religious quotations were also included. Many of the sayings were original.

Colors

Norwegians are said to have a special "gift" for color. Green, blue, gold, and red are colors typically used in rosemaling. One main color is used in the design. Blue is used most often. Other colors, along with black and white, are used to fill in the pattern.

Waiting for Luraas

Thomas Luraas was Telemark's most famous rosemaler. It is said that people in Hardanger kept unfinished trunks around for as long as seven years, hoping he would show up and paint something on them.

Colorful rosemaling ▶ patterns decorate even common household objects.

Tools

- good quality acrylic paintbrushes; #2, 4, & 6 flat, #2 & 6 round brushes with long tips (liners or scrollers) *(See diagram.)*
- large water container
- paint rag
- pencil
- ruler
- flat wooden surface (a box, cutting board, etc.)
- small plastic container with lid

Rosemaling Brushes

flat

round (liner or scroller)

Materials

- wax paper
- acrylic paints: cadmium red (light), alizarin crimson, raw umber, Prussian blue, yellow ochre, white, ivory, black
- acrylic gloss medium
- white paper
- sandpaper
- white latex enamel paint
- transfer paper

You can paint decorative designs on any wood surface. Begin by learning the basic forms. Then you'll be ready to plan your own combinations.

Experiment with Color Mixing

Rosemaling colors have a special look. Each base color is toned down with a neutral color, such as raw umber or white. Authentic rosemaling is painted with oil paints, but acrylic paint is safer to use. The gloss medium gives acrylics a luster that is similar to oils. Try mixing the Norwegian colors described below.

1. Read the acrylic paint hints on this page. Mix the colors one at a time on a piece of wax paper. Squeeze out a small dab of the base color. Add an equal amount of acrylic gloss medium. Add a very tiny amount of each toner color.

2. Dip a brush in water, and then use it to blend the paints well. Test the color on a piece of white paper. Experiment by adding a bit more toner color. Test the color again. Take your time and get familiar with the different combinations.

3. Traditional background colors are red, black, white, and blue. Paint a small patch of each on white paper. When the colors are dry, test other colors on top of them. *(See Norwegian Colors box.)*

Acrylic Paint Hints

- Protect your clothing with an old shirt or a smock. When acrylic paint is still wet, it can be removed with water. Once it dries, it cannot be removed.

- Acrylics dry quickly. Mix only a small amount of each color. If the paints begin to dry out, moisten them with a little water.

- Before using a new color, rinse the brush well and wipe it on a rag.

- Never let paint dry in a brush. When you are finished painting, wash the brushes thoroughly with soap and water.

Norwegian Colors

red – cadmium red (toned with alizarin crimson and raw umber)

blue – Prussian blue (toned with raw umber and white)

gold – yellow ochre (toned with raw umber and white)

green – Prussian blue plus yellow ochre (toned with white)

black – ivory black (toned with raw umber)

white – white (toned with raw umber)

Experiment with Brush Strokes

Begin by learning some basic brush strokes. Practice making the flower, leaf, and the other shapes described here. Feel free to repeat each stroke many times, until it looks smooth and fluid. Good brushes are very important to achieve the results you want. Use the best brushes you can afford.

Flowers and Leaves

1. Flowers and leaves are painted with a flat brush. Dip your brush into water. Push it back and forth in the paint, working it into the hairs. Then smooth the brush by wiping each side on the wax paper. Reload the brush in this way for each stroke.

2. First, practice a full circle stroke, used for flower centers. Hold the brush straight up and down. With a steady downward pressure, twist the brush slowly around in a full circle. One brush tip stays in the center and the other moves around the outside edge. *(See diagram.)*

3. When you complete the circle, spiral the brush a little way into the center, as shown. Gradually release the pressure and lift the brush. Make several more full circle strokes, with different sizes of flat brushes. *(See diagram.)*

4. Next, draw a simple rounded petal with a pencil, like the example shown. Paint the whole petal with one flowing stroke. Begin at the base. Stroke up to the top, then twist the brush with your fingers. Let one tip of the brush move smoothly around the top edge. Pull the stroke back to the base, ending next to where you started. *(See diagram.)*

5. Flower petals come in many shapes and sizes. Use a narrow brush for small petals and a wide brush for large petals. For a wide flower petal with a narrow base, begin the stroke up on one tip of the brush. Then increase the pressure to fill the wide part of the shape. *(See diagram.)*

6. Now, draw a leaf with an S-shaped edge. A leaf is usually painted with more than one stroke. Paint along the S-shaped edge first, beginning at the top and stroking down to the base. Next paint the other edge. Then fill in the center. Use the brush that will fill the shape with the fewest strokes. *(See diagram.)*

Practice the brush strokes on ▶ paper before you plan your project.

Flowers and Leaves

2. Practice a full circle stroke.

3. Complete the circle stroke.

4. Practice a rounded petal stroke.

base

5. Make some flower petals.

6. Practice making a leaf shape.

7. Complete some flower and leaf designs.

Long Strokes and Details

2. Make a C-shaped scroll.

3. Add branches to the scroll.

4. Practice making flower stems.

5. Add outlines.

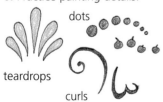

6. Practice painting details.

dots

teardrops

curls

7. When you have practiced all the strokes, try some of the complete flower and leaf designs shown here. Read Painting Flowers and Leaves. *(See diagram.)*

Long Strokes and Details

1. Smaller details and long strokes, such as scrolls, stems, and outlines, are usually painted with a round brush. Dip the brush into water. Roll it over and over in the paint until it is well loaded. Smooth the brush back into a point on the wax paper.

2. Scrolls are shapes that look like thick vines. They are used to connect and fill between the flowers. Draw a C-shaped scroll. Paint it in one long, smooth stroke. Paint up from the bottom, along the inside edge. Stroke around the large rounded top. Then paint back to the bottom along the outside edge, gradually easing the pressure. *(See diagram.)*

3. Add graceful branches to the scroll using the same stroke. *(See diagram.)*

4. Paint flower stems with a small round brush. Start at the bottom. Draw the brush slowly up to the flower in a flowing curve. Increase and decrease the brush pressure to change the thickness of the stem and make it lively. Practice until you can paint graceful stems in any direction. *(See diagram.)*

5. Outlines are the thin lines added to the outside edges of flowers, leaves, and scrolls. They help to make the shapes stand out. They are painted in just the same way as flower stems. Use brush pressure to make flowing changes from thick to thin. *(See diagram.)*

6. All kinds of little detail strokes are painted with a round brush. Practice making different sizes of teardrops, dots, and curls. *(See diagram.)*

Painting Flowers and Leaves

■ When strokes overlap, begin at the outside with the leaves, and work in to the flower center. (Follow the numbers on the illustration.)

■ Let each part dry before you continue so that the colors don't get muddy.

■ Turn the paper as you work, so that the petal or leaf you are painting points up.

Plan Your Design

Now you are ready to decorate something with rosemaling! Find a wooden surface to paint. Anything smooth and flat will work, like an old wooden box or a cutting board. You can find many old wooden objects at yard sales and secondhand stores.

1. Plan your design. Look at pictures of Norwegian rosemaling in this book and in other books. Pick out small areas that you like from a larger design. Read the Design Hints on this page. Then make a small sketch of your ideas.

2. Trace around the wooden object to make a pattern of the space you will fill. Draw a design that looks balanced and strong. Take your time. Fill the area well, so not much empty space is left. *(See diagram.)*

3. Decide on the background color and the other colors you'll use for parts of the design. Look back at your original color tests to help decide on combinations. Label all the colors on the pattern. *(See diagram.)*

4. Plan the order to paint each part of the design. Start on the outside of a design and work toward the center. This way, you will cover over the rough edges of ending strokes. *(See diagram.)*

5. Practice painting your design on paper. Place a piece of transfer paper on the paper, with your pattern on top. To transfer the design, trace over the outlines of the bigger shapes. *(See diagram.)*

▼ Decorate a wooden object with rosemaling.

6. Mix the colors you will use. Paint the bigger shapes of the design on the paper. Then add the outlines and details. Examine the results. If you aren't totally satisfied, paint the design again. The more you practice, the happier you will be with the end product.

Design Hints

■ The central shape of a rosemaling design is usually a large scroll or flower. Smaller flowers, leaves, and scrolls grow out of this central shape.

■ Fit the design to the space you are decorating. Small spaces look best filled with small, delicate forms. Large spaces need bold forms.

■ Use each color in several different places in the design so that it will have a unified, or whole, look.

Plan Your Design

2. Make a pattern.

3. Label the colors.

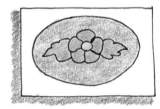

4. Plan the order of the strokes.

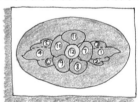

5. Transfer the design.

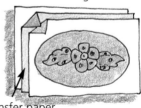

transfer paper

Other Ideas

■ Experiment with blending two colors in one brush stroke.

■ After you get more practice, decorate a larger surface, such as a chair, chest, or a mirror frame.

Decorate with Rosemaling

5. Transfer the pattern.

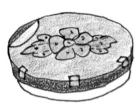

Decorate with Rosemaling

1. Prepare the wood surface. If you are using an old wood object, take the time to clean and sand it well.

2. Paint the surface with white enamel paint. When the enamel is dry, sand it again.

3. Mix the background color in a small plastic container. Mix plenty of this color, because it's hard to match if you run out. Use an equal amount of gloss medium to create a glossy finish on your wood.

4. Paint the background color with long, smooth strokes. Paint all in one direction. Let the wood dry again. Apply a second coat if necessary. Cover and save the leftover paint to use if needed for touch-ups.

5. When the paint is completely dry, transfer the pattern to the wood surface with transfer paper. *(See diagram.)*

6. Paint the design as you practiced it. Read the suggestions in the Rosemaling Hints box to remind you of some basics.

7. When all the bigger shapes are painted, finish the outlines and details. Not every edge needs an outline. Too many outlines will make the design look boring.

8. Remember, part of the appeal of rosemaling is that it is painted freely. A lopsided flower has charm, and crooked scrolls are just fine. However, if you are unhappy with a stroke, make a new stroke quickly before the paint dries. Or, wipe the stroke off quickly with a damp cloth.

Rosemaling Hints

■ When strokes overlap, begin at the outside and work toward the center.

■ Wait for each part of the design to dry before painting over it, or the colors will smear and become dull.

■ Turn the object as you work, so that you can make the brush stroke in the best direction.

Three rosemaling projects ▶ designed and painted by students.

Glossary

ancestors descendants, people who have gone before

Arctic Circle the region that lies about 66 degrees north of the equator, where for a time in summer the sun never sets and in winter it never rises

artisans people who are skilled in an art, a craft, or a trade

bilingual speaking two languages

embroidery decorative needlework

emigrate leave one's residence or country to live elsewhere

ethnic relating to racial, national or cultural background

fjord narrow inlets of the sea between cliffs or steep slopes

glacier large body of ice moving slowly down a slope or valley

gnome in folktales, a small figure who lives underground and guards the earth's treasures

indigenous native to or the original inhabitants of a region

marathon a long-distance foot race of 26 miles (67.40 km)

medieval referring to the Middle Ages (A.D. 1000 to 1400)

migration moving from one place to another, often seasonally

mythology ancient stories used to explain natural events

nomadic moving seasonally from place to place; having no fixed place of residence

plateau a level land surface raised sharply above land next to it on at least one side

ritual a series of actions regularly followed, especially in a religious ceremony

supernatural appearing to be beyond what is normal or able to be explained by the laws of nature

tundra a treeless plain that is characteristic of the Arctic, with permanently frozen subsoil

Abbreviation Key

sq.	square
mi.	miles
km	kilometers
ft.	feet
m	meters
in.	inches
cm	centimeters
F	Fahrenheit
C	Centigrade
g	grams

Resources

Norway

Kagda, Sakina, and Rudolf Steiner. *Norway,* "Cultures of the World" series. New York: Benchmark, 1996

Miller, Margaret M., and Sigmund Aarseth. *Norwegian Rosemaling: Decorative Painting on Wood.* New York: Charles Scribner's Sons, 1974

Zickgraf, Ralph. *Norway,* "Major World Nations" series. Broomall, PA: Chelsea House, 1997

Sweden

Carlsson, Bo Kage. *Sweden,* "Modern Industrial World" series. Austin, TX: Raintree Steck-Vaughn, 1995

Klein, Barbro, and Mats Widbom, eds. *Swedish Folk Art: All Tradition Is Change.* New York: Harry N. Abrams, 1994

Zickgraf, Ralph. *Sweden,* "Major World Nations" series. Broomall, PA: Chelsea House, 1997

Denmark

Bengtsson, Gerda. *Gerda Bengtsson's Book of Danish Stitchery.* New York: Van Nostrand Reinhold, 1972

Lerner Publications, Department of Geography Staff. *Denmark in Pictures,* "Visual Geography" series. Minneapolis, MN: Lerner, 1997

Nielson, Edith. *Scandinavian Embroidery: Past and Present.* New York: Charles Scribner's Sons, 1978

Lapland

Beach, Hugh. *A Year in Lapland: Guest of the Reindeer Herders.* Washington, DC: Smithsonian, 1993

Manker, Ernst. *People of Eight Seasons: The Story of the Lapps.* New York: Viking, 1963

Vitebsky, Piers. *Saami of Lapland,* "Threatened Cultures" series. Austin, TX: Raintree Steck-Vaughn, 1994

Index

Acknowledgments

Special thanks to these students for their time and energy in making the project samples: Breeze, Carrie B., Carrie S., Jessica, Martina, Quail, Sanya, and Tim; and to Arias for his help. Thanks also to Patterson Family School, Eugene, Oregon; Barb Shirk; Louis Carosio; Mary Lou Finigan; Jean Anderson; Einar and Marilyn Skovbo; Tristan Franklin; Diane Cissel, Terragraphics; Libris Solar; City Copy; Percy Franklin; Stephen Reynolds; and Wade Long. Thanks to the Eugene Public Library and the Salt Lake City Public Library reference librarians for their ongoing help.